MW00990873

THE ART OF
EXALTED™

ARTISTS

Tazio Bettin
Ed Bourelle
Mark Brooks
Leanne Buckley
Ross Campbell
Eric Canete
Trevor Claxton
Misty Coats
Danimation
Samuel Donato
Meghan 'Sebychu' Donbrowski
Newton Ewell
John Floyd
Dave Gonzales
Groundbreakers Inc.
Andrew Hepworth
Jeff Holt
HOON
Hyung-Tae Kim
Saana 'Kiyo' Lappalainen
Kevin Lau
David Leri
Vince Locke
Justin Norman
Aaron Norell
William O'Connor
Pasi Pitkanen
Chris Stevens
EJ Su
Mark Anthony Taduran
Joshua Gabriel Timbrook
Andie Tong
Melissa Uran
Long Vo
Mark Joseph Vivas
Eva Widermann

Imaginary Friends Studio (Sami Basri, Boon, Kevin Chin, Erfan Fajar, Fiduciose, Sunny Gho, Sinad Jaruartjanapat, Buddy Jiang, Lan Jun Kang, Pilvi Kuusela, Kendrick Lim, Kenneth Loh, Rhoald Marcellius, Arif Priyanto, Tabitha Reed, Yatawee Rutsameecharoen, Djoko Santiko, Scabrouspencil, Dani Siswadi, Skan Srisuwan, Sudathip Techakriengkrai, Elda The, Ray Toh, Kierston VandeKraats, Adimira Wijayadi, YJL, Zhi Xian and Theresa Zysk)

Pat Lee and Dreamwave Productions with matt milberger

UDON (with Atilla Adorjany, Eric Annette, Greg Brown, Greg Boychuk, Roberto Campus, Christine Choi, Steven Cummings, Omar Dogan, Espen Grundetjern, Andrew Hou, Scott Hepburn, Eric Kim, Herbert Kwan, Leo Lingas, Jorge Molina, Joe Ng, Ryan Odagawa, Charles Park, Francisco Perez, Ramon Perez, Noi Sackda, Mark Sinclair, Chris Stevens, Pierre Theriault, Arnold Tsang, Eric Vedder, Adam Vehige, Joe Vriens, Alan Wang, Kevin Yan, Gary Yeung and Jim Zubkavich)

Adam Warren (with Lee Duhig, GuruFX and Ryan Kinnaird)

Authors: John Chambers and Brian Glass
Editor: Carl Bowen
Creative Director: Rich Thomas
Production Manager: matt milberger
Art Direction: Brian Glass
Layout: matt milberger

WHITE WOLF PUBLISHING
2075 WEST PARK PLACE BOULEVARD
SUITE G
STONE MOUNTAIN, GA 30087

WELCOME TO THE ART OF EXALTED.

This book represents a labor of love on the part of Brian Glass and myself. We have been working on **Exalted** since 2001, and in that time, we've seen a ton of spectacular art go into this game. Given the nature of our business, the art is often buried in parts of books that are referenced infrequently or obscured by text, banners or logos. In this book, though, we put that art front and center to stand on its own merits.

As first imagined, **Exalted** was to be illustrated like a standard fantasy game of the period, though admittedly by a bunch of talented folks who had a history of creating quality art for White Wolf Publishing: Guy Davis, Chris Moeller, Vince Locke, Jeff Holt, Leif Jones, Joshua Gabriel Timbrook and others. Rather than settle for what was the norm in gaming at that time, however, **Exalted's** creators and their bosses—Geoff Grabowski, matt milberger, Rich Thomas, Ken Cliffe and Steve Wieck—decided to take a chance with something different. Whether they were riffing on the post-millennial zeitgeist or could foresee the rise of manga and anime in American popular culture, these guys decided at the eleventh hour that going with an art style encompassing (but not limited to) Eastern manga was the thing to do. In the second edition, Brian and I pushed the manga ties even further, introducing opening manga for each chapter of the game's releases.

Now, over eight years and nearly 70 releases later, the art of **Exalted** has become a style in its own right, influenced by the technique of Asian comics without simply mimicking it. And it's also introduced a lot of incredible talent to the game industry through the use of studios such as Dreamwave Productions, UDON, Imaginary Friends and Groundbreakers, Inc., as well as individual artists such as Melissa Uran, Adam Warren, Ross Campbell, Chris Stevens and Hyung-Tae Kim, to name just a few. As we continue to publish supplements, Brian and I will keep pushing the artistic quality of **Exalted**. I hope you fans will always be with us to see it, because none of what we do would be possible without you. Thanks for eight great years.

The best is yet to come.

John Chambers

Ah, **Exalted**. I still remember looking at the original layout with matt and getting the approval to start contacting "anime and manga" style artists to change the look of the book. It was the first time I know of that we'd ever completely changed graphical direction of a game line so close to sending it to athe printer. It was extremely exciting. I grew up watching Battle of the Planets (a.k.a. Gatchaman), Bubblegum Crisis and tons of others. It was so cool to be able to help bring that change about. It was even more exciting when I was given free reign to art direct **Exalted**.

Brian Glass

Exalted Second Edition
UDON

Exalted Second Edition
Imaginary Friends Studio

Exalted Second Edition
UDON

Exalted Second Edition
Imaginary Friends Studio

Legacy of the Unconquered Sun
Dave Gonzalez

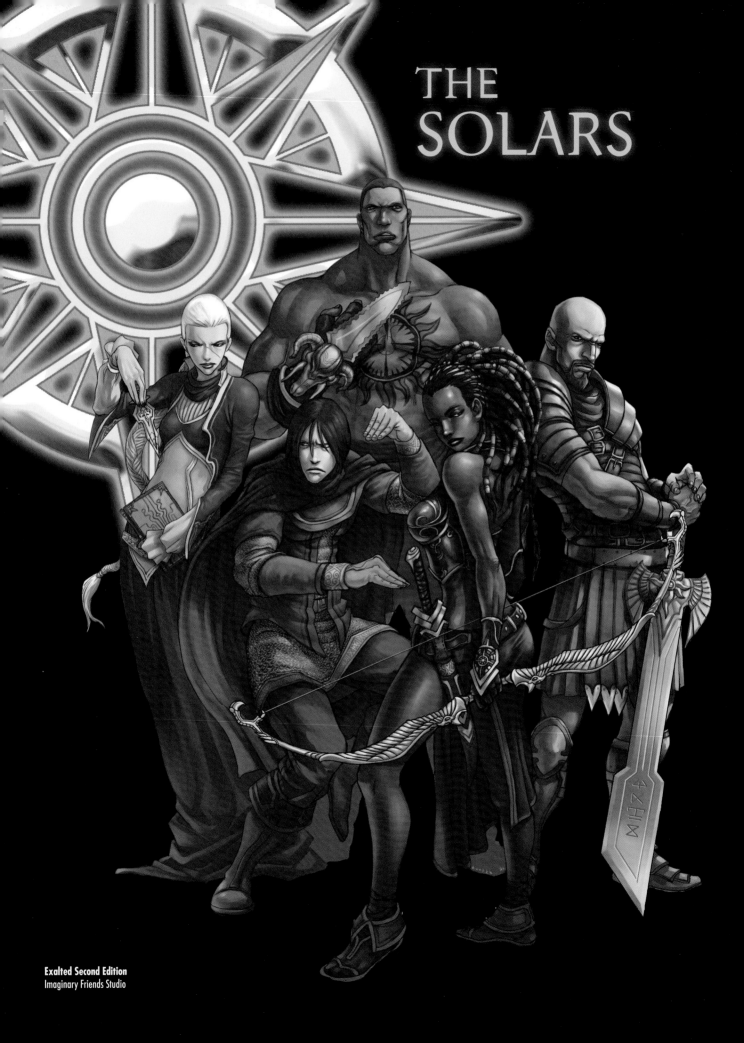

THE SOLARS

Blessed by the Unconquered Sun, the most powerful of the gods, these mighty Lawgivers ruled Creation for millennia by the authority of the Mandate of Heaven. Yet the Great Curse of their ancient enemies caused them to grow increasingly paranoid and insane as their power increased. In time, their fearful Sidereal Exalted advisors saw no alternative but to orchestrate a bloody coup. The ambitious Dragon-Blooded carried out the Sidereals' orders, and their Usurpation brought the wondrous Old Realm to an end. The Essences of the slain Solars were long imprisoned, but now they are free to find and empower new heroic souls. Reborn Lawgivers stride the world once more, growing into untold power and threatening the status quo by their very existence.

Five castes of Solar Exalted exist: the Dawn Caste warriors, the Zenith Caste priests, the Twilight Caste savants, the Night Caste spies and the Eclipse Caste diplomats. As the mightiest and most glorious of the Exalted, the Solars are poised to retake Creation and turn it into a paradise more glorious than the halcyon days of the First Age. Their Charms lead the Solars naturally to perfection in every endeavor, and their gleaming weapons of orichalcum strike fear into the hearts of all creatures of darkness. Many threats stand poised to destroy Creation, however—not the least of which is the abiding madness of the Great Curse within the Solars' hearts.

Exalted First Edition
Pat Lee and Dreamwave Productions (with matt milberger)

We first got in touch with Pat back for the first edition core book. He and Dreamwave helped set an excellent starting point, which we've built on ever since. I remember matt and I hanging out with Pat and some of his crew years ago at Chicago Comicon (before it was Wizard World Chicago). We were looking through his sketchbook and saw several different versions of Harmonious Jade as he was working his way up to illustrating the cover of the book. It was really cool to see "behind the scenes" like that.

– BG

Exalted Second Edition
Andrew Hepworth

Exalted First Edition
William O'Connor

Caste Book: Dawn
Chris Stevens

ARIANNA
TWILIGHT CASTE

An intelligent young woman employed as a menial servant in a library of misogynist scholars in the North, Arianna was thrilled by the intellectual freedom being Exalted as a Twilight Caste offered her. At last, she could delve into the knowledge so long kept from her by the library's scholars. Her knowledge soon surpassed theirs, leading her to a growing mastery of sorcery. Jealousy and fear led those selfsame academics to inform the Dragon-Blooded Wyld Hunt of Arianna's Anathema status and whereabouts. The scar on her face serves as a constant reminder of the dangers that outed Solars face in the Age of Sorrows. It was during her flight from the Wyld Hunt that Arianna first encountered her circlemate Swan, and the two have been close ever since.

In Northern Twilight
UDON

Exalted Second Edition
Melissa Uran

**The Books of Sorcery, Volume II —
The White and Black Treatises**
Antie Tong

Exalted Second Edition
UDON

The Book of Three Circles
David Leri

DACE
DAWN CASTE

The Dawn Caste hero Dace is a veteran mercenary captain who grew up an orphan in the camps of the Ravenous Wolves company and later joined the mercenaries as a career soldier. His entire life served to prepare him for his Exaltation on the field of battle and his concomitant role as a warrior and general in the service of the Unconquered Sun. Dace now dwells in the sprawling city of Nexus. There, he divides his time between serving the city's ruling Council of Entities as the head of the Bronze Tigers mercenary company and lending his orichalcum blade to the cause of protecting Creation during this Time of Tumult with his circle of Solar allies.

My method of art directing varies per artist. For some of my newer people, I try to give more specific art notes, just to make sure they draw our characters and can get a good feel of the setting. For some of the more "regular" artists on the line, I try to give more creative freedom. I'll send the artists several sections of text and let them choose which part to illustrate. I'll then go in and make sure that what they're drawing matches up to what's been written. I try to be accommodating to my artists and their work style while still overseeing the project and making sure the art fits the text.
– BG

Relic of the Dawn
UDON

Exalted Card Game
UDON (with Chris Stevens)

Exalted Second Edition
UDON

Caste Book: Dawn
Chris Stevens

The Compass of Terrestrial Directions, Volume I — The Scavenger Lands
UDON

HARMONIUS JADE
NIGHT CASTE

Sold to the Southern Salmalin Yozi cult soon after birth and raised as one of that organization's premier assassins, Harmonious Jade was Exalted as a Night Caste during a botched assassination. When she returned to the only home she'd ever known for instructions after this profound development, the Salmalin set upon her and tried to kill her. (After all, the Solar Exalted were the ones who had originally defeated and imprisoned all demonkind.) After a desperate and bloody escape, Jade fled the South with vengeful cultists in hot pursuit, pausing only long enough to collect the orichalcum powerbow she now carries from the tomb of her First Age predecessor. Searching for purpose to her Exaltation, the deadly Solar comes to the attention of Dace, who brings the murderous naïf into his growing circle.

Man, who doesn't like a kick-ass assassin, raised by demon cultists and then becoming a Chosen one? Everything about Harmonious Jade is cool. She's always been one of my favorite characters to have illustrated in the game line. Strong, powerful, bad-ass and sexy.
– BG

A Day Dark As Night
UDON

Exalted Second Edition
UDON

Legacy of the Unconquered Sun
Imaginary Friends Studio

Exalted First Edition
Pat Lee

I love this visual origin of Harmonious Jade, from being sold to the Yozi cult, to a childhood of training, to her earliest assassination, to her fleeing the cult after her Exaltation, to Jade the Night Caste Exalt of the present. It's all told beautifully and quite effectively in only five tiny panels.

– JC

PANTHER
ZENITH CASTE

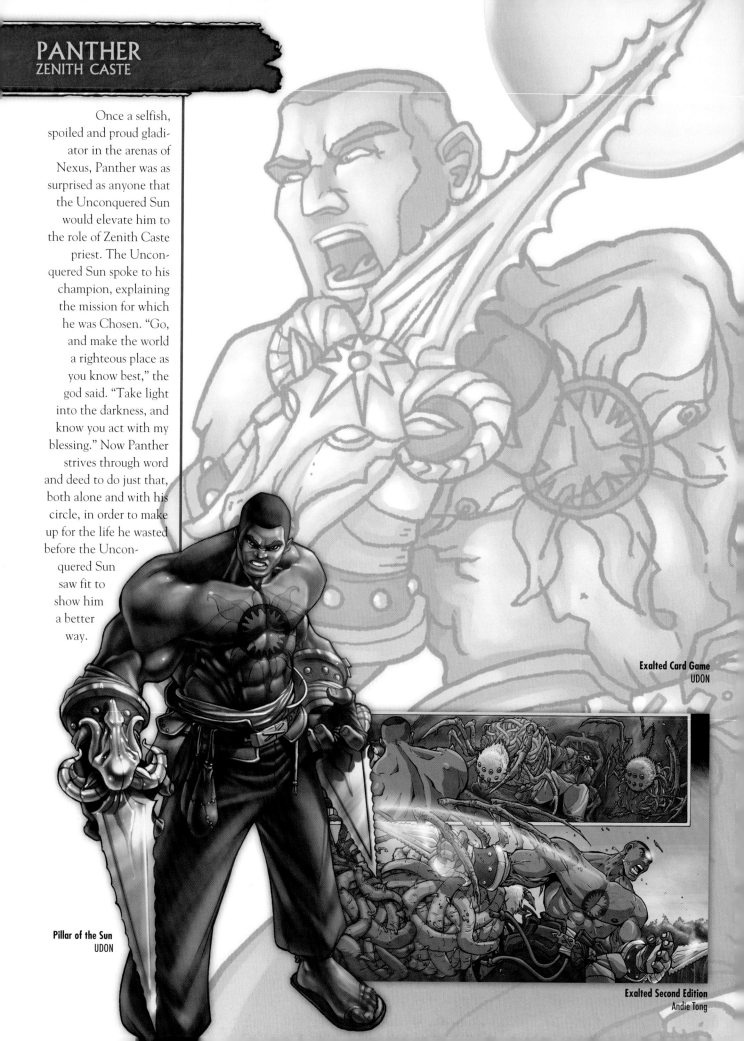

Once a selfish, spoiled and proud gladiator in the arenas of Nexus, Panther was as surprised as anyone that the Unconquered Sun would elevate him to the role of Zenith Caste priest. The Unconquered Sun spoke to his champion, explaining the mission for which he was Chosen. "Go, and make the world a righteous place as you know best," the god said. "Take light into the darkness, and know you act with my blessing." Now Panther strives through word and deed to do just that, both alone and with his circle, in order to make up for the life he wasted before the Unconquered Sun saw fit to show him a better way.

Exalted Card Game
UDON

Pillar of the Sun
UDON

Exalted Second Edition
Andie Tong

Caste Book: Zenith
Chris Stevens

Exalted Second Edition
Andie Tong

SWAN
ECLIPSE CASTE

A junior member of the diplomatic corps of the West's Coral Archipelago, Swan was Exalted as an Eclipse Caste when, while on a diplomatic mission in the North, he came across Arianna being pursued by the Wyld Hunt. Leaping in to protect the wounded woman, heedless of the danger to himself, Swan found himself empowered with the strength and skill at martial arts he needed to save her. Swan has since devoted his diplomatic skill and his noble heart to protecting the interests of Creation as a whole rather than those of any one nation. In so doing, he has proved a worthy addition to his circle time and again.

A Shadow Over Heaven's Eye
UDON

Originally, these characters were sketched out by Rich Thomas and then given to Melissa Uran to polish up for our art bible. Since then, we've had a solid design of our signature characters and have been able to get lots of talented artists to give us their takes on them. It's nice as an art director to be able to get so many cool minor variations on our core characters. One of these days, Dace might actually try on some pants.

Ross Campbell, Chris Stevens and Melissa Uran were fantastic in setting the original look and style of Exalted. They really got the game and nailed it early on. I'm thankful for having such instrumental artists able to work for me.

—BG

Scroll of the Monk
UDON (with Chris Stevens)

Legacy of the Unconquered Sun
Imaginary Friends Studio

Legacy of the Unconquered Sun
Imaginary Friends Studio

Legacy of the Unconquered Sun
Imaginary Friends Studio

Legacy of the Unconquered Sun
Imaginary Friends Studio

Legacy of the Unconquered Sun
Imaginary Friends Studio

Legacy of the Unconquered Sun
Imaginary Friends Studio

Exalted Second Edition
UDON

Legacy of the Unconquered Sun
Imaginary Friends Studio

The Manual of Exalted Power — The Infernals
Groundbreakers Studio

THE DRAGON-BLOODED

The Manual of Exalted Power — The Dragon-Blooded
UDON

The least individually powerful but most populous of the Exalted, the Dragon-Blooded derive their power from the Five Elemental Dragons, representing the elements of Air, Earth, Fire, Water and Wood. Ever since the end of the First Age, when they threw down their former masters in the Usurpation, these Terrestrial Exalted have ruled Creation. Successive Dragon-Blooded Shogunates reigned for generations, until the Fair Folk beyond Creation's borders launched the Balorian Crusade—an all-out campaign of genocide and mass destruction. The hopes of humanity dimmed until a lone Dragon-Blooded hero single-handedly turned the tide of battle and saved Creation. In the seven-plus centuries since that time, she has built a world-spanning Scarlet Empire, also known simply as the Realm, which she rules as the Scarlet Empress. Under her, a mighty Dynasty of eleven Great Houses has grown to rule the vast majority of the world directly and extort tribute from almost everyone else.

With Charms based on the five elements of Creation, as well as a surviving magitechnical infrastructure and huge numbers of Terrestrial Exalts who grow more powerful by working in concert, the Dragon-Blooded constitute the chief threat facing the returned Solar Exalted. Yet the Scarlet Empress has mysteriously disappeared of late, and the Great Houses are in disarray over the question of succession. The reborn Lawgivers might yet wrest the reins of Creation from the Terrestrial Exalted— if so, though, it'll likely be over their shattered jade blades.

SCIONS OF THE SCARLET DYNASTY

The Dragon-Blooded Dynasts of the Scarlet Empire are a varied lot of demigods, as evinced by these six examples. The portly Wood-aspected Nagezzer the Slug is publicly disparaged for his crippled body and wastrel lifestyle, but he secretly works to maintain the Realm and stave off a civil war between the Great Houses. The Water Aspect Peleps Deled is a fanatical monk and member of the Wyld Hunt who believes there is but one true interpretation of the Immaculate faith—his own. Then there are the two possible successors to the vanished Scarlet Empress. The Roseblack, a Wood-aspected soldier, is the inheritor of the Empress's fighting spirit. Mnemon, an Earth-aspected sorceress, is the Empress's eldest daughter by blood. Finally, there are the young Fire-aspected soldier Avaku of Ways and the disgraced Air-aspected general Tepet Arada. Avaku is just beginning his military career, while Arada is striving to walk away from his responsibilities in the wake of personal tragedy.

War for the Throne
Imaginary Friends Studio

TEPET EJAVA, THE ROSEBLACK
WOOD ASPECT
War for the Throne
UDON

**MNEMON
EARTH ASPECT**
Aspect Book: Earth
Kevin Lau (with UDON)

War for the Throne
Imaginary Friends Studio

**TEPET ARADA
AIR ASPECT**
Aspect Book: Air
Kevin Lau (with UDON)

War for the Throne
Imaginary Friends Studio

The Dragon-Blooded have always been very iconic antagonists for the Solars.

In my mind, they're the overpowering authority, desperately trying to hang on to a crumbling rule. When we created these guys, we knew they were going to get their "powers" from the Elemental Dragons, so we assigned colors to each aspect. Blue for air, white with a tinge of purple for earth, red for fire, black for water and green for wood. We did similar things for the Sidereals, the Alchemicals and the Fair Folk. There are distinct colors based on either the characters or where their powers come from. Each Exalt type is also "assigned" a cover color. The Solars get the golden rice paper. Dragon-Blooded get a deep, regal red. The Lunars get a cool blue, reminiscent of the moon. The Abyssals get a mottled black. The Sidereals get a royal purple. The Fair Folk get a deep forest green. The Alchemicals get a dark, rusty texture. The Infernals get a nice bronze. If you look at the Compass of Celestial Directions books, it's easy to immediately see what overall subject the book is about by looking at the background color.

– BG

Aspect Book: Fire
Andie Tong

**CYNIS DENOVAH AVAKU OF WAYS
FIRE ASPECT**
War for the Throne
UDON

PELEPS DELED
WATER ASPECT

Exalted: The Dragon-Blooded
Pat Lee and Dreamwave Productions

SESUS NAGEZZER, THE SLUG
WOOD ASPECT

Aspect Book: Wood
Kevin Lau (with UDON)

War for the Throne
UDON

Exalted Second Edition
Melissa Uran

This is an awesome piece, the first time in the game's history, other than concept art, where we had illustrated the Five Elemental Dragons who are the source of the Dragon-Bloods' power.

— JC

Aspect Book: Fire
Eva Widermann

Exalted: The Dragon-Blooded
Melissa Uran

Exalted: The Dragon-Blooded
William O'Connor

The Compass of Celestial Directions, Volume 1 — The Blessed Isle
UDON

Exalted: The Dragon-Blooded
Pat Lee and Dreamwave Productions (with matt milberger)

I'm fond of this piece, as it represents one of only two instances in the entire **Exalted** run where we show the Scarlet Empress on her throne, leading Creation as she did for nearly eight centuries. Since her absence from the setting is one of the central plot points of the game, there had just seldom been a reason to show it. But I think the piece does a great job of conveying a sense of the woman's power and dignity.

– JC

Exalted Second Edition
Imaginary Friends Studio

Time for an inside joke. John and I have been getting "Winghead" (the gentlemen with the wings on his helmet) illustrated since **Exalted's** second edition core. Poor fellow's had his eye shot out, he's been stabbed, he's been blown up, he's been turned into a hungry ghost… I heard a rumor that he might actually get stats in an upcoming book. I love any excuse to have him show up. He's just a fun, hapless character we like to abuse. See how many books you can spot him in.

– BG

THE LUNAR EXALTED

Once mates of the Solar Exalted, the Chosen of Luna abandoned the Lawgivers during the Usurpation and fled to the fringes of Creation to brood and plot the downfall of the traitorous Dragon-Blooded and their Sidereal puppet-masters. After the Lunars nearly lost themselves to the chaotic power of the Wyld, their elders devised a series of intricate moonsilver tattoos to stabilize their shapes and minds. The elders' efforts bulwarked the Lunars against destruction, but at the cost of two of their original castes. Thereafter, there were but three: the savage Full Moons, the mysterious No Moons and the mercurial Changing Moons. These Stewards of Creation now seek to bring about a new world order, having spent centuries devising alternatives to the governments of both the ancient Lawgivers and the modern Dragon-Bloods. With the Realm edging toward civil war, now is the perfect time to strike… if the rebirth of the Solar mates they once abandoned doesn't give the Lunars pause.

Legacy of the Unconquered Sun
Andrew Hepworth

This scene of the ancient Lunar Exalt Leviathan swimming in the dark depths of the Western Ocean past the sunken First Age metropolis of Luthe has been interpreted by a number of artists in both editions of the game, but this version is perhaps the most hauntingly beautiful.
– JC

STEWARDS OF CREATION

The shapeshifting Chosen of Luna play many roles. These four, however, serve to exemplify their castes. Anja Silverclaws is a No Moon spy who seeks to uncover the secrets of the Deathlords. Red Jaws is a Changing Moon hunter and slayer of Creation's enemies, the Fair Folk and the dead. Strength of Many, once a slave himself, uses the power of the Full Moon to punish those who would rob others of their inherent freedom. And finally there's Madame Vert, a Lunar with no fixed caste, who has yet to be initiated into the Silver Pact and has yet to have her shape fixed by the moonsilver tattoos of the Pact's elders.

**ANJA SILVERCLAWS
NO MOON CASTE**

**MADAME VERT
CASTELESS**

RED JAWS
CHANGING MOON CASTE

STRENGTH OF MANY
FULL MOON CASTE

The Manual of Exalted Power — The Lunars
Saana 'Kiyo' Lappalainen

Kiyo did an incredible job on these signature characters. We introduced a new one in **The Manual of Exalted Power—The Lunars,** and Kiyo managed to make a lizard woman crazy sexy. I personally think these are some of the best-looking Lunars we've seen to date.

– BG

The Manual of Exalted Power — The Lunars
Saana 'Kiyo' Lappalainen

Exalted: The Lunars
Chris Stevens

Legacy of the Unconquered Sun
Mark Joseph Vivas

The Manual of
Exalted Power
— The Lunars
Saana 'Kiyo' Lappalainen

Exalted: The Lunars
Chris Stevens

Dreams of the First Age
Misty Coats

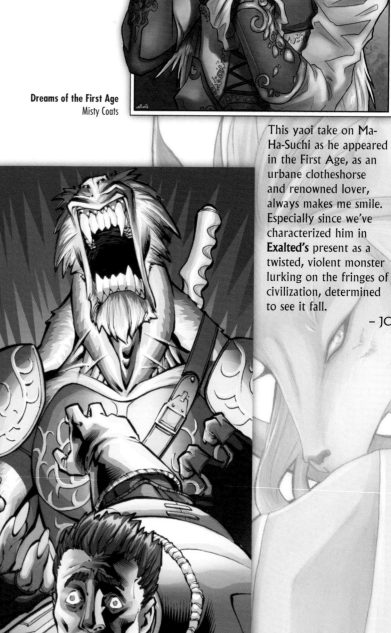

This yaoi take on Ma-Ha-Suchi as he appeared in the First Age, as an urbane clotheshorse and renowned lover, always makes me smile. Especially since we've characterized him in **Exalted's** present as a twisted, violent monster lurking on the fringes of civilization, determined to see it fall.

— JC

The Manual of Exalted Power — The Lunars
Long Vo

The Manual of Exalted Power — The Lunars
Ross Campbell

Exalted Second Edition
Imaginary Friends Studio

Exalted: The Lunars
William O'Connor

THE ABYSSALS

The Manual of Exalted Power — The Abyssals
Imaginary Friends Studio

The rebirth of the Lawgivers has come at a price, for not all of the Essences that once empowered the Chosen of the Unconquered Sun have returned to Creation. One hundred Essences were stolen by the evil Deathlords, powerful ghosts of thirteen Solar Exalts slain in the Usurpation. The Deathlords serve the horrific Neverborn, twisting the Solar Essences they possess to reflect and suit their masters' purposes. The undying deathknights whom these corrupted Essences empower are called the Abyssal Exalted.

The Abyssals' castes mirror those of the Solars, with Dusk Caste warriors, Midnight Caste priests, Daybreak Caste savants, Day Caste spies and Moonshadow Caste diplomats. Outfitted with panoplies of moaning soulsteel, these morbid Exalts ride forth from the lands of the dead on a mission to end all life and bring the Neverborn's gift of Oblivion to Creation. As prone to perfection as their Solar opposites and supported by armies of the dead, little can stand against the Chosen of the Void on their dark crusade. Their main limitation is their inability to thrive on the wholesome life energy of the lands of the living… and the guttering glimmer of Solar heroism that still exists deep within all Abyssals' souls.

A Day as Dark as Night
UDON

KNIGHTS OF DEATH

Handpicked by the Deathlords to do their bidding, these Abyssal Exalts are twisted reflections of the Solar castes on which they are based. The Lady of Darkness in Bloodstained Robes is the Midnight Caste high priestess of an ancestor-worshiping cult intended to empower the dead and draw more ghosts to the Deathlords' banner. The brilliant Daybreak Caste Seven Degreed Physician of Black Maladies devotes himself to the creation of necrotech war machines designed to slay the living in vast numbers, thus providing him with even more corpses to work into new abominations. The Dusk Caste general called the Maiden of the Mirthless Smile yearns to unleash the full undead might of the Deathlords against the unsuspecting Scavenger Lands so that she can test her mettle against that of Creation's greatest warriors. The Essence of the unstoppable Day Caste assassin the Disciple of the Seven Forbidden Wisdoms once belonged to the lover of Harmonious Jade's First Age incarnation, which has occasionally led to conflicts of interest costly to each others' causes. Lastly, Falling Tears Poet is a Moonshadow Caste diplomat attempting to unite the Underworld's many servants of Oblivion and keep them from working at cross-purposes.

THE LADY OF DARKNESS IN BLOODSTAINED ROBES MIDNIGHT CASTE

FALLING TEARS POET MOONSHADOW CASTE

THE MAIDEN OF
THE MIRTHLESS SMILE
DUSK CASTE

THE DISCIPLE OF THE SEVEN
FORBIDDEN WISDOMS
DAY CASTE

THE SEVEN DEGREED PHYSICIAN
OF BLACK MALADIES
DAYBREAK CASTE

Exalted: The Abyssals
Melissa Uran

Exalted: The Abyssals
UDON

Legacy of the Unconquered Sun
Samuel Donato

I remember like it was only a year ago — well, it was about a year ago as of this writing — 2007 New Years vacation. A bunch of us were in a cool house up in the mountains of Tennessee. It was snowing. I brought **The Manual of Exalted Power — Abyssals** along to work on.

I convinced my "New Years' Blood Helper Monkeys" to suck ink into coffee stirrers and then blow it all over paper so we could make all the blood smears in that book. I have about 30 pages of runny blood and blood splatters now. My mouth might have wound up black, but it was a lot of fun spraying "blood" onto paper out on the porch in the snow.

– BG

Legacy of the Unconquered Sun
Samuel Donato

I dig Ross's take on the bow of screaming doom and the reanimatory aftereffects of its usage. The characters are pure Ross, with **piercings galore and animal bones and prayer strips for clothing,** but that twisted soulsteel bow and the carved-bone arrows it's fired through the forms of its poor victims… that's really disturbing.
– JC

The Book of Bone and Ebony
Ross Campbell

Exalted: The Abyssals
UDON

This illustration by Joe Vriens is, to me, one of the finest at conveying the crazy frenetic feel of combat and stunting in the game.
– JC

Exalted Storyteller's Companion First Edition
Ross Campbell

I actually grossed myself out while working on the first edition Abyssals book. I wanted to give the sidebars and Charm trees an almost skin-like texture. In order to do this, I manipulated images of body modification and scarification and branding. Man, those were some unpleasant pictures to work with, but I love the results.
– BG

Exalted: The Abyssals
Leanne Buckler

The Books of Sorcery,
Volume III — Oadenol's Codex
UDON

Exalted: The Abyssals
William O'Connor

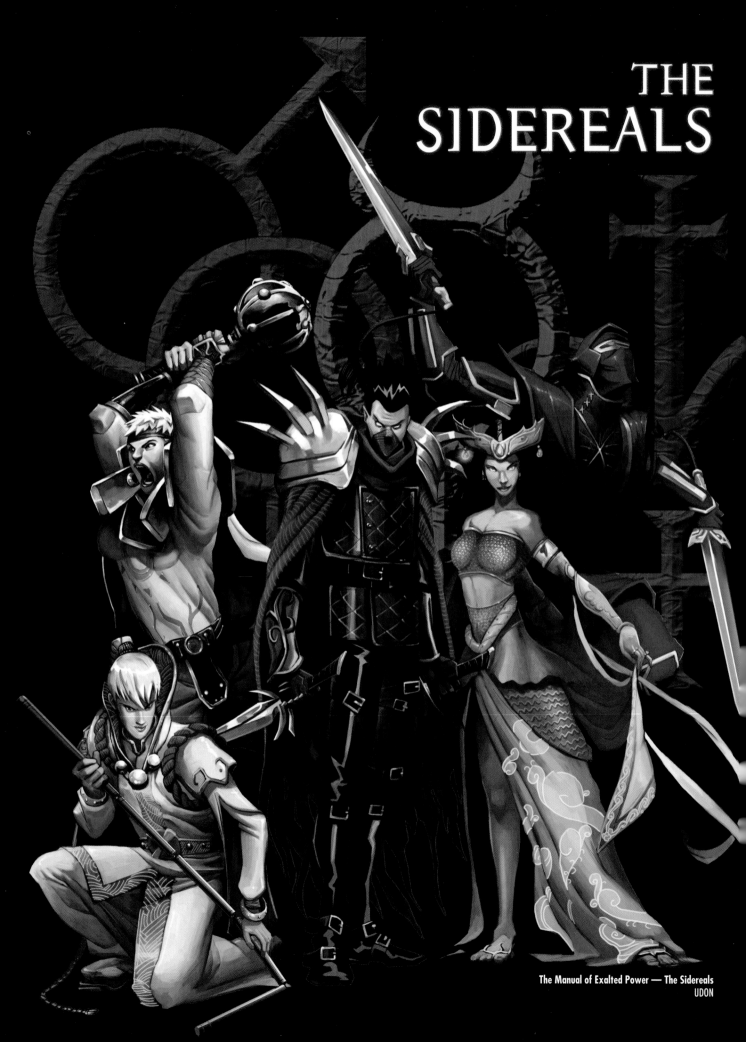

THE SIDEREALS

Essences forever imprisoned for the good of Creation, the Maiden's Chosen incited the Dragon-Bloods to strike the Solars down. To hide their involvement in the Usurpation, the Sidereals then damaged the stars themselves and seemed to fade from existence.

Exälted Second Edition
Melissa Uran

Since that time, the Sidereal Exalted have hidden themselves from history and manipulated Creation from behind the scenes using their command of astrology and fate-based Charms. They repurposed the Immaculate Order as a tool to brand the Solar and Lunar Exalted "Anathema" and organized the Wyld Hunts to eliminate said Anathema. The five castes of Sidereals—the Chosen of Journeys, of Serenity, of Battles, of Secrets and of Endings—devote the majority of their efforts toward righting snarls in the weave of fate, often fighting incursions from without by demons and the Fair Folk. Many Exalted, however, have also met their end at the hands and starmetal weapons of these consummate martial artists.

AGENTS OF DESTINY

Destined for Exaltation at birth and employed by Heaven's Bureau of Destiny, these five Exalts are each mired in the current highly charged political climate in which all Sidereals find themselves.

A Chosen of Battles, the mysterious Crimson Banner Executioner is involved with the Sidereal Gold Faction's efforts to put the Solars back into positions of power (with appropriate oversight by the Maidens' Chosen, of course). Iron Siaka is a Chosen of Serenity demon-hunter and a notorious rake, sometimes seducing the very women she's saved from demon attack. Nominally loyal to the Sidereal Bronze Faction, Siaka has no head for politics and holds little against the Solar Exalted. Black Ice Shadow was an experiment by Heaven to raise a Sidereal agent from birth in conditions that would allow him to better understand the Deathlords and their goals, an experiment that worked so well his superiors now believe the Chosen of Endings might be compromised. May Blossom is a Chosen of Secrets and a loyal proponent of the Bronze Faction, which has dominated Sidereal politics since the Usurpation. For his part, the Chosen of Journeys Shepherd of the North Star does his best to avoid the internecine politics of the Sidereals, wishing his fellows would spend less time trying to outmaneuver one another and more time handling the growing list of threats to Creation's well-being.

**BLACK ICE SHADOW
CHOSEN OF ENDINGS**

SHEPHERD OF THE NORTH STAR
CHOSEN OF JOURNEYS

CRIMSON BANNER EXECUTIONER
CHOSEN OF BATTLES

The Manual of Exalted Power — The Sidereals
Trevor Claxton

IRON SIAKA
CHOSEN OF SERENITY

MAY BLOSSOM
CHOSEN OF SECRETS

Legacy of the Unconquered Sun
David Gonzalez

Exalted: The Sidereals
Ross Campbell

Legacy of the Unconquered Sun
David Gonzalez

Exalted: The Lunars
Mark Brooks (with UDON)

Cult of the Illuminated
UDON

Exalted: The Sidereals
Ross Campbell

Exalted: The Sidereals
Chris Stevens

This illo of Chejop Kejak does a great job of getting across the Sidereal elder's age and wisdom. It shows just how heavily the many hard decisions this central figure of Creation's history has had to make in the past, and those he's going to have to make about the future, weigh on the man. It's a terrific piece of art.
– JC

Exalted First Edition
David Leri

Exalted: The Sidereals
Andie Tong

Exalted: The Sidereals
William O'Connor

THE FAIR FOLK

Before Creation was formed, all that existed was the chaos of the
Wyld and the formless raksha who dwelt within it. Capricious and immortal, the raksha played elaborate games of dominance and submission
for an unknowable period, as time was but one of many things yet to be
created. When the horrible static machine of Creation was spun out of
the boundless potential of the Wyld, however, the raksha were forever
changed. Now, instead of an infinity of pure chaos, there was something
else. That something defined the raksha as not of it, which intrigued,
confounded and even angered them. Yet they could do nothing about it
at first, as its static nature calcified and killed those raksha who crossed
its borders. This state of affairs persisted until the raksha learned how
to build solid bodies for themselves—similar to those of Creation's
mortals—which could contain and protect their formless souls. They also
learned how to batten themselves on the chaos of mortal dreams in order
to survive in Creation indefinitely. They have existed as a bane on the
shaped world ever since. Fearful of invoking these powerful supernatural
predators through the use of their true name, Creation's mortals have
named them the Fair Folk.

LORDS OF CHAOS

These four raksha nobles exemplify the threat posed to Creation's people by the predatory Fair Folk. A raksha Artisan, Dilari of the Sea Foam draws men to their doom in Creation's West, as they drown themselves to be with her. Shikuzi the Weaver is a Scribe of and advisor to the South's Ruby Court. The beautiful cloth he weaves from the hair of still-living human captives brings misfortune to those who would wear it. Neshi of the Double Whips is the Imperial Raksha who rules the Southern Lapis Court. She surrounds herself with an entourage of human children whom she dotes on and protects, until they invariably displease her and she cruelly dispatches them while the others look on. The Laughing Boy of the East's Opal Court is the very definition of a raksha Anarch, racing barefoot through the Wyld trailing fire in his wake only to enter Creation on a whim to tear people and dwellings apart with his clawed hands.

SHIKUZI THE WEAVER
NOBLE WORKER

DILARI OF THE SEA FOAM
NOBLE ENTERTAINER

Exalted: The Fair Folk
Melissa Uran

NESHI OF THE DOUBLE WHIPS
NOBLE DIPLOMAT

THE LAUGHING BOY
NOBLE WARRIOR

I love this piece. I still remember when I got the final illustration. It was around the holidays last year, I was back home visiting the family with my fiancée (wife now). My folks still have dial-up, so I drove to the town square to check my email using the town's wi-fi. I downloaded the cover and was just blown away with how gorgeous it looked. I immediately forwarded it to John and called him and made him promise to check his email as soon as he got home. This is one of my favorite covers. Seriously, this was an extra Christmas present.

– BG

Graceful Wicked Masques — The Fair Folk
Imaginary Friends Studio

For the raksha, I've always tried to play up natural elements and the chaotic nature of the Wyld. That's why I broke the standard layout in **Exalted: The Fair Folk** and again in **Graceful Wicked Masques.** Instead of having the usual character strip of art, I had the artists break the frames and bleed the art off the page and slowly straighten back into the strict frame to show the Fair Folk basically "leaving" the Wyld and "entering" Creation. You see a similar thing when you look at **The Compass of Celestial Directions, Vol. II—The Wyld.** Instead of just having the character popped out and placed on the front, like the rest of the books, I have him trailing fire from the illustration, as though he's leading the procession out of the frame of the art. It's way more subtle than on the other two books, but still there.

– BG

The Compass of Celestial Directions, Volume II: The Wyld
UDON

Kingdom of Halta
Melissa Uran

Graceful Wicked Masques — The Fair Folk
UDON

Graceful Wicked Masques — The Fair Folk
Melissa Uran

Examples by Melissa Uran of Fair Folk commoners from each of the cardinal directions: an ophidian Entertainer from the East, an owlish Diplomat from the North, a sharkman Warrior from the West and a leonine Worker from the South. These illustrations are all based on pieces provided by artist Jeff Holt years ago for the **Exalted** art bible.

– JC

Aspect Book: Wood
Pasi Pitkanen

Graceful Wicked Masques — The Fair Folk
John Floyd

Graceful Wicked Masques — The Fair Folk
UDON

THE
ALCHEMICALS

As the Solars grew more decadent and mad in the First Age, their onetime ally Autochthon, the Primordial Great Maker, retreated from Creation for fear that the Lawgivers would eventually turn against him. He took with him his many subordinate lesser machine gods and millions of mortal worshipers. Since that time, these refugees have dwelled within the Great Maker's very body, protected from harm by mighty champions known as the Alchemical Exalted. These vat-born golems with the souls of heroes grow in size as they grow in power, with the largest forming the very cities in which the Autochthonian people dwell. Alchemicals are melded with Charms built from the magical materials during their creation process, leading to the five common castes of Alchemicals: Jade, Orichalcum, Moonsilver, Starmetal and Soulsteel (as well as an apocryphal sixth Adamant Caste). It normally falls to the Alchemicals to face only those threats that exist within Autochthon's failing body. Yet, as supplies in the Autochthonian nations run low after millennia in isolation, the Alchemical Exalts must now lead the bravest of Autochthonian mortals into Creation to procure what their people need to survive.

CRUSADERS OF THE MACHINE GOD

Products of vast Alchemical vat complexes, these Exalts are born to serve a specific function in Autochthonian society. The Soulsteel Caste Alchemical Dreadful Adjudicator of Law acts as an enforcer of policy and hunter of dissidents. Lissome Avid Engineer is a Starmetal Caste architect, machinesmith and engineer. Fair-Spoken Rishi of the Orichalcum Caste is master of Autochthonian politics, though he rose to fame initially based upon his popularity as a war hero. Those warrior skills remain sharp even now, hundreds of years later. The lithe Moonsilver Caste Excessively Righteous Blossom was built for war. Unfortunately for his many subordinates, the overzealous Blossom is much better suited to single combat than to commanding troops. The powerful Jade Caste Alchemical Stern Whip of Industry, meanwhile, was designed to handle industrial accidents and provide emergency services in case of infrastructural collapse.

DREADFUL ADJUDICATOR OF LAW
SOULSTEEL CASTE

LISSOME AVID ENGINEER
STARMETAL CASTE

EXCESSIVELY RIGHTEOUS BLOSSOM
MOONSILVER CASTE

STERN WHIP OF INDUSTRY
JADE CASTE

FAIR-SPOKEN RISHI
ORICHALCUM CASTE

Exalted: The Autochthonians
UDON

Exalted: The Autochthonians
Ross Campbell

Exalted: The Autochthonians
Melissa Uran

Exalted: The Autochthonians
Jeff Holt

Exalted: The Autochthonians
UDON

Exalted: The Autochthonians
UDON

Time of Tumult
Chris Stevens

This is the piece that first introduced me to artist Chris Stevens, a guy whose work is now synonymous in my mind with the look of **Exalted.**

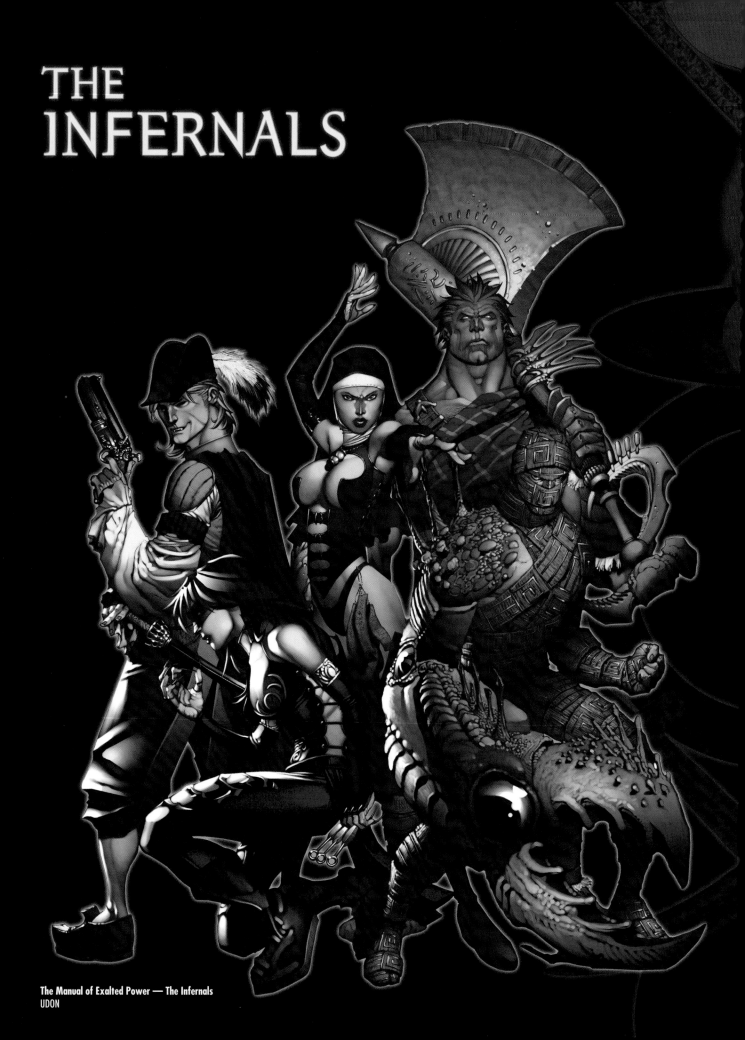

THE INFERNALS

To escape destruction at the hands of the ancient Lawgivers, the malevolent Yozis surrendered to the Solars and were cast into Hell beneath the glaring light of an awful green sun. Forever separate from Creation, they could still corrupt that which they could lure or capture. Among their conquests were mortals, Dragon-Bloods and even Solars—all of whom they rebuilt into insidious akuma slaves. In an effort to learn the Yozis' secret methods, the Neverborn made a deal. They would have their Deathlords free the Solar Essences imprisoned at the end of the Usurpation and tithe fifty to the Yozis in Hell. In return, the Yozis would share the secret of corrupting a Solar Essence. Once this exchange was carried out, a coalition of five Yozis rebuilt the fifty Solar Essences to absorb and convert the energy of Hell, rather than that of Creation.

The Yozis then gifted these Infernal Essences to failed mortal heroes, creating and laying claim to five castes of Infernal Exalted. The castes include the brutal Slayers, who serve Malfeas; the blasphemous Malefactors, who revere Cecelyne; the clever Defilers, who venerate She Who Lives in Her Name; the subtle Scourges, who emulate Adorjan; and the duplicitous Fiends of the Ebon Dragon. No mere akuma slaves, these Green Sun Princes wield tarnished relics and command demonic servants, carrying out a plan to forge Creation into Hell and free the Yozis from their millennia-long exile. The Green Sun Princes fit the description of the "Anathema" the Immaculate Order warns of and often take advantage of that fact to cast the reborn Lawgivers in a bad light.

Exalted Second Edition
Ross Campbell

HEROES OF HELL

These five failed heroes and their two-score-and-five Infernal brethren represent perhaps the greatest extant threat to Creation. Operating among the Lintha family of the west, Bitter Copal is an ingenious Defiler Caste builder of helltech devices, including his own fourfold demon arm. The Scourge Caste Captain Gyrfalcon is a swashbuckling sky pirate preying on Northern air boats and settlements. Cearr is a savage Slayer spreading destruction and pain throughout the Far East. Under the guise of a scion of House Nellens, the Fiend Manosque Cyan intends to avenge the Manosque family on the Scarlet Dynasty that wiped it out. And finally, Sulumor, the Malefactor Caste Infernal also known as the Wan Stavrophore, uses religious conviction to turn the Southern dune people into an army in the service of the Yozis.

SULUMOR, THE WAN STRAVROPHORE
MALEFACTOR CASTE

CAPTAIN GYRFALCON
SCOURGE CASTE

MANOSQUE CYAN
FIEND CASTE

CEARR
SLAYER CASTE

BITTER COPAL
DEFILER CASTE

CREATION

The Skullstone Archipelago

Onyx

Azure

The Coral Archipelago

The Neck

The Great Western Ocean

Abalone

The Wavecrest Archipelago

Eagle's Launch

The Blessed Isle

Lo Cro

Arjuf

City of the Steel Lotus

Bluehaven

The L

Gem

Raised from the Wyld by the will of the Primordials, Creation was designed to form a bulwark against the Wyld's chaos, offering both shelter (in the form of static reality inimical to the Wyld) and sustenance (in the form of its denizens' prayers). Having built this fortress, the Primordials created the gods to maintain it and then withdrew to the heavenly realm of Yu-Shan to play their Games of Divinity. Alas, the gods betrayed their masters, turning lowly mortals into Exalted heroes who could take up arms against the Primordials where the gods could not. After a long and costly war, the Primordials were brought low. Those who were slain—now called the Neverborn—were cast to the brink of Oblivion, where they yet linger. Those who surrendered—now called Yozis—swore crippling bindings and were imprisoned far from Creation. Well pleased with their Exalted champions, the gods retired to Yu-Shan to take their leisure and play the Games of Divinity themselves. They laid down the Mandate of Heaven, which offered the Exalted dominion over Creation as spoils of battle, and the world has remained under Exalted control ever since.

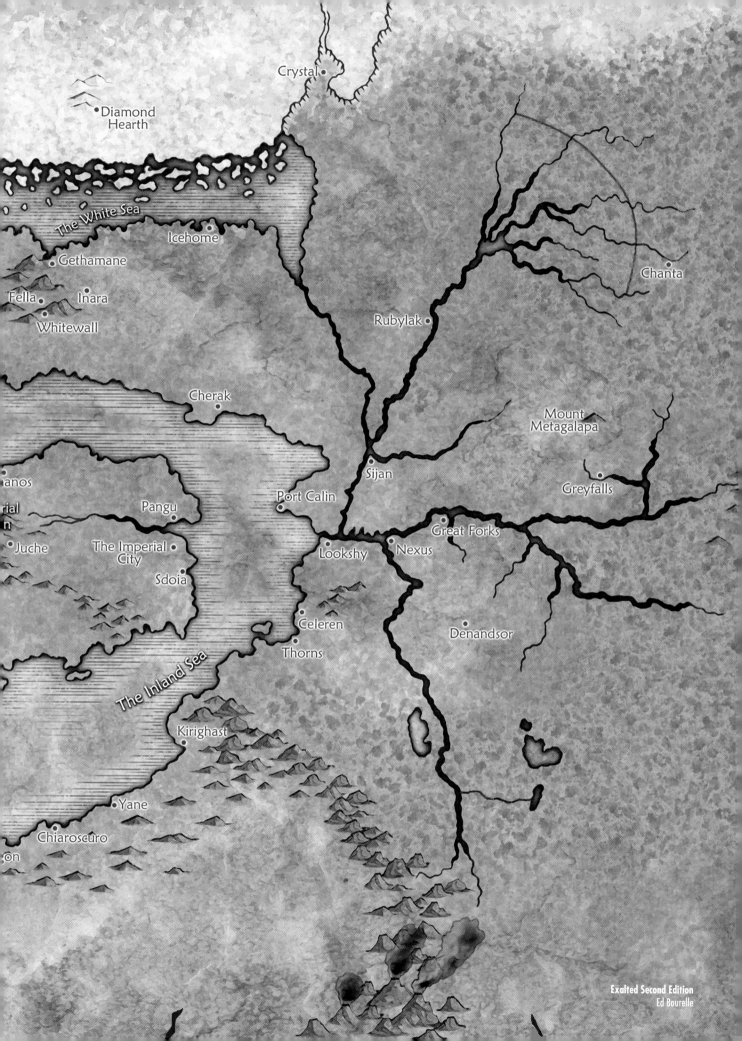

Crystal

Diamond
Hearth

The White Sea

Icehome

Gethamane

Fella   Inara

Whitewall

Chanta

Rubylak

Cherak

Mount
Metagalapa

...anos

...rial
...n

Pangu

Sijan

Greyfalls

...Juche

The Imperial
City

Port Calin

Sdoia

Great Forks

Lookshy   Nexus

Celeren

Denandsor

Thorns

The Inland Sea

Kirighast

Yane

Chiaroscuro

...on

The Blessed Isle lies perfectly at the center of all the five elements' confluence, enjoying a perfect climate. In addition, as the center of the Scarlet Empire, it has not known war in nearly eight centuries.

The Compass of Celestial Directions, Volume I — The Blessed Isle
Imaginary Friends Studio

I just love the statue on this cover. The weathered look, the black roses starting to grow on it as if implying that the Roseblack, Tepet Ejava, would soon be taking over as Empress. I also love how you see the Imperial City in the background, looking very tiny, but regal. Compare that to the sprawling, grandiose city of Meru from the cover of **Dreams of the First Age**. A very different look and feel between the past and the present, yet taking place at basically the same location (Meru was on the mountain's top, while the Imperial City is at its base).

– BG

I remember the original of this piece used to hang outside of original **Exalted** Developer Geoff Grabowski's office before the first edition was released and how psyched this image got me. So psyched, in fact, that I walked right into my boss's office and declared I wanted to be the one to edit that game.

-JC

Exalted First Edition
Vince Locke

Dreams of the First Age
UDON

Dreams of the First Age
UDON

To me, this single panel conveys all one needs to know to understand why the legions of the Scarlet Empire dominated warfare in Creation for over 700 years. Check the intensity in the eyes of the heavy legionnaire on the far left.

This is not a military force one wants to provoke.

– JC

Exalted: The Dragon-Blooded
Chris Stevens

This illustration of a Northern town whose inhabitants have just vanished manages to convey both the stark beauty of the place and the sinister aspect of how the folk went missing. The spelling out of the name of the unshaped raksha responsible on the sides of the central post in Old Realm script is a really cool touch, alluding to the word "Croatoan" carved into a post that was the only clue to the disappearance of the Lost Colony of Roanoke.
– JC

Bastions of the North
Andrew Hepworth

THE NORTH

Across the Inland Sea and the Great Western Ocean from the Blessed Isle lies Creation's Threshold. The North, home to the Elemental Pole of Air, is a region of wind, ice and snow. Containing the nations of Whitewall, Gethamane, the Haslanti League and Cherak, along with countless barbarian tribes, the land grows ever harsher as one travels northward. Finally, it falls away entirely to reveal an expanse of cold blue sky alone.

Exalted Second Edition
UDON

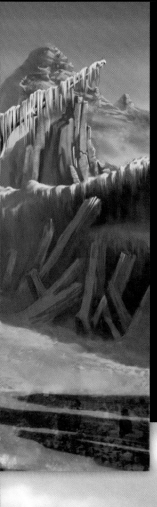

Whenever I need a wicked location, I turn to
Andrew Hepworth. Andy continues to turn in
some truly beautiful work, from the cool locations
found in the **Legacy of the Unconquered Sun** board
game to the insane cover of the Fair Folk attacking
the Haltans in **The Compass of Terrestrial Directions, Vol. III — The East**. Andy's gorgeous architecture really helps define the world of **Exalted**.

– BG

Legacy of the Unconquered Sun
Andrew Hepworth

In Northern Twilight
UDON

THE EAST

The most populous and productive of the cardinal directions, the East's fecundity is attributable to its proximity to the Elemental Pole of Wood. A huge expanse of territory, the East encompasses thousands of kingdoms, city-states, duchies, principalities, satrapies and other forms of government, including Linowan, Metagalapa, the Republics of Halta and Chaya and the tomb-city Sijan, before ending in its farthest reaches as an impenetrable expanse of trees. Also present in the East is a coalition of nations that, despite their prosperity, have successfully avoided the Scarlet Empire's dominance for almost 800 years. This coalition calls itself the Confederation of Rivers; others disparagingly refer to its aggregate as the Scavenger Lands. Supported by the military powerhouse Lookshy, the Scavenger Lands consist of the economic hub Nexus, the temple city Great Forks, the rustic Celeren and a hundred other nations besides.

This two-page cover illustrates an assault by the Fair Folk on the Eastern tree city of Chanta. Andrew Hepworth's attention to detail and his sense of design make this piece a favorite of mine.
– JC

The Compass of Terrestial Directions, Volume III —The East
Andrew Hepworth

Legacy of the Unconquered Sun
Andrew Hepworth

Scavenger Sons
Leanne Buckley

Kingdom of Halta
UDON

Ruins of Rathess
Kevin Lau (with UDON)

Here we have a cool piece showing the nations of the Confederation of Rivers coming together to protect the sprawling city of Nexus from attack. The mercenaries of Nexus are seen standing side by side with the ashigaru and gunzosha troops of military powerhouse Lookshy, while warstriders tower over the common troops and skyships fly overhead. Also, the outline of the Emissary can be seen enveloping the city that lies under the aegis of his protection.

– JC

One of the few
illustrations of the
Scavenger Lands
city-state of Lookshy,
with a junk's-eye view
up from the harbor.
— JC

Scavenger Sons
Leanne Buckley

A Shadow Over Heaven's Eye
UDON

Exalted Second Edition
UDON

Legacy of the Unconquered Sun
Andrew Hepworth

Here we have a view of the extant First Age
Southern city of Chiaroscuro meeting its final end
under the blazing Godspear of another
First Age holdover, the Five-Metal Shrike,
its imperishable glass towers melting to slag.
– JC

The Compass of Terrestial Direction, Volume IV — The South
UDON

Exalted Second Edition
UDON

THE SOUTH

The South is an arid region of tremendous heat. Away from the temperate
cities that lie on its coast —Yane, Kirighast, Paragon, the Lap and
Chiaroscuro —the land turns to desert, and the heat and volcanic activity
increases the farther south one travels until one reaches the Elemental
Pole of Fire itself, an endless expanse of colorless flame.

Manacle and Coin
Andie Tong

The Compass of Terrestial Directions, Volume II — The West
Ross Campbell

Manacle and Coin
Ross Campbell

The Books of Sorcery, Volume III — Oadenol's Codex
HOON

Scroll of Kings
Pasi Pitkanen

To let you folks in on a little secret, being the game's developer means you can have your own character illustrated on the cover of an **Exalted** supplement.
– JC

THE WEST

Finally, the West is home to a myriad of islands and archipelago nations strung like pearls across the neck of the Great Western Ocean. Ships of the Coral Archipelago, the Neck, Bluehaven, the Wavecrest Archipelago and Skullstone all ply the waves of the West. Sailors must be ever mindful as they journey closer to the Elemental Pole of Water and the endless devouring Sea. Beyond it lies only the formless Wyld, where there be things far worse than dragons.

This illustration depicts a savage battle between the Lintha pirates and the Realm navy, with the Realm's Dragon-Blooded captain employing an artifact Essence lash against famed Lintha outcaste Haquen Ronkevool, whose proficiency with his jade blade, Flicker-Fang, has kept him from harm.

– JC

Blood and Salt
Melissa Uran

Exalted Second Edition
Andrew Hepworth

Exalted Second Edition
UDON

THE WYLD

Beyond the borders of static Creation lies the endless maddening expanse of chaos that is most properly termed the Wyld. At the world's outer elemental poles, however, this pure chaos melds with the edges of reality to form a mercurial land of limitless possibility… and danger. Interacting with the nearest elemental pole, the Wyld is home to bizarre elemental phenomena and wondrous prodigies, as well as to the courts of the Fair Folk, tribes of mutated barbarians and the Lunars' savage beastman offspring. Even if one avoids the lands' many overt dangers, it is easy to become addicted to the subtle promise of the Wyld to alter and improve oneself. Most mortals return from time spent in the Wyld changed in mind and body.

The goddess Luna has some measure of influence over the Wyld. In the dark of the new moon, the tide of the Wyld recedes. When the moon shines brightly overhead, however, the Wyld surges forth to engulf areas normally free of its influence. Knowledgeable folk living at Creation's fringes give Wyld zones a wide berth at such times.

Exalted Second Edition
Pasi Pitkanen

This piece depicts an apocryphal story where one of the central figures of the Realm's Immaculate faith, Daana'd, the Dragon of Water, confronted the Queen of the Deep Wyld in order to seal the chaotic horrors she birthed forever outside Creation.

– JC

Exalted Second Edition
Melissa Uran

Graceful Wicked Masques — The Fair Folk
Priscilla Kim

Graceful Wicked Masques — The Fair Folk
John Floyd

THE UNDERWORLD

Here we see five of the Deathlords looking on as one of their number, the Dowager of the Irreverent Vulgate in Unrent Veils, summons forth the Great Contagion from the depths of the Well of Udr.

— JC

The Book of Bone and Ebony
UDON

The Compass of Celestial Directions, Volume IV — The Underworld
Melissa Uran

Souls once reincarnated upon death without exception, but now there exists a place where those with unfinished business might be drawn by the dark gravitas of the Neverborn. That place the Underworld, came into being at the moment the first of the Neverborn was slain in the Primordial War. The very impossibilit of such a demise caused a dark and turbulent mirror of Creation to be fashioned to house its dead Primordial architects. The dead-but-dreaming Neverborn spirits dwell there still, their tombs lining the Well of the Void, which lies at the brink of ultimate Oblivion.

In the Underworld, the collective memories of departed humar souls have shaped a world much like the one they left behind There they play at living and stave off reincarnation, never losing themselves to the forgetfulness of Lethe. Just as the deaths of the Neverborn first tore through the fabric of Creation, other heinou acts that result in widespread death can tear holes in Creation leaving gaping wounds into the Underworld. Through these wounded places, called shadowlands, ghosts and worse things car return from beyond death to plague the lands of the living.

Exalted Second Edition
Imaginary Friends Studio

**The Compass of Celestial Directions,
Volume IV — The Underworld**
Imaginary Friends Studio

Exalted Second Edition
UDON

The Books of Sorcery, Volume II — The White and Black Treatises
Imaginary Friends Studio

The Manual of Exalted Power
— The Abyssals
UDON

Exalted: The Abyssals
Ross Campbell

The Books of Sorcery, Volume V
— The Roll of Glorious Divinity II
Imaginary Friends Studio

The Compass of Celestial Directions, Volume IV — The Underworld
Melissa Uran

Exalted: The Abyssals
Ross Campbell

MALFEAS

The Yozis, those Primordials who laid down their arms at the end of the Primordial War, were broken in body and spirit and forced to swear dreadful oaths of surrender on their names. The body of their king was turned inside out, and the Yozis were forced inside and banished to dwell in the prison of their own crippled forms for eternity. Is it any wonder that the name of the Yozi king, Malfeas, who encompasses his fellows, is synonymous with the term Hell?

A raucous world of sickly green light and unearthly din, Malfeas is unlike Creation in that its every inhabitant, its every physical feature, is but a part of the greater Yozis who make up the world. With little else to do, the Yozis and their subordinate souls, the Demon Princes, crafted whole races of lesser demons to inhabit their prison realm. These cruel and monstrous beings are tied by the oaths their progenitors swore to remain in Hell unless properly summoned to Creation, where they must do the bidding of the Exalted who conquered them. Like any prison, the demon realm of Malfeas is a violent place where the frustrations of the strong are taken out on the weak—a state of affairs the Yozis are determined to inflict on the folk of Creation the moment they break free.

The Compass of Celestial Directions, Volume V — Malfeas
Groundbreakers Studio

The Books of Sorcery, Volume V — The Roll of Glorious Divinity II
UDON

I love the Malfeas realm.
Evil-looking demons, sexy neomah,
grotesque-yet-gorgeous, architecture.
What's not to love?

You'll get a better look at this nefarious realm in **The Manual of Exalted Power — The Infernals** and **The Compass of Celestial Directions, Vol. V — Malfeas.** I have to say that I'm really excited about these two projects. I love letting my artists push their dark sides, and I'm still really fond of both versions of **Abyssals** and the Underworld book. We're going to have lots of twisted fun in the Malfean realm.

– BG

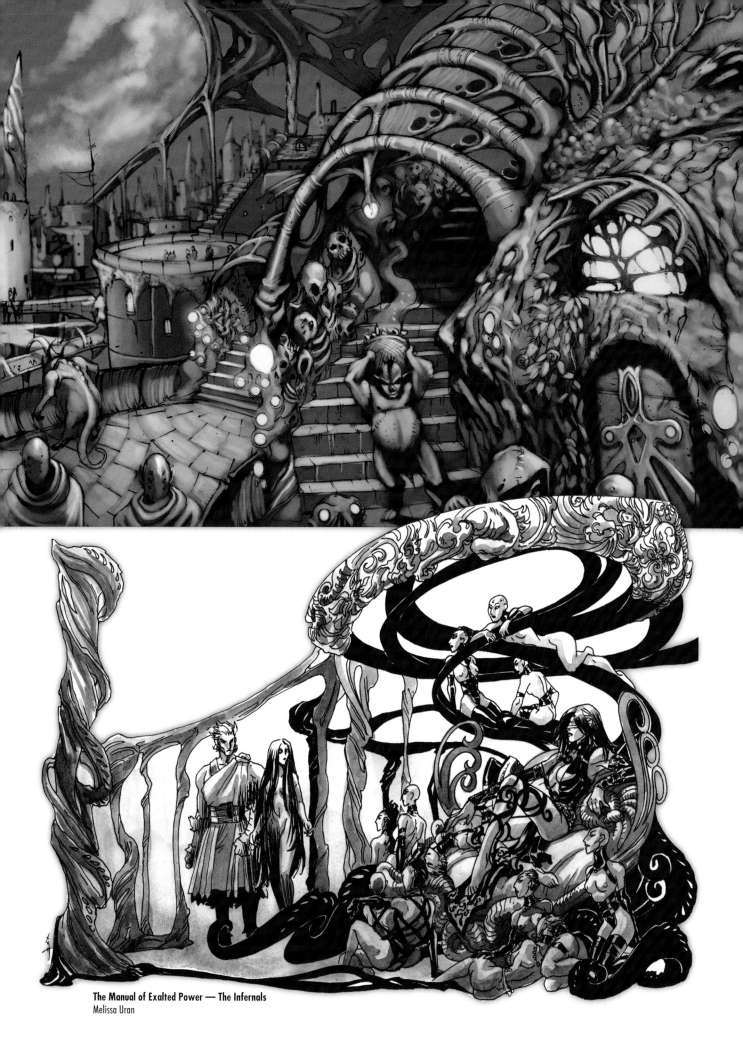

The Manual of Exalted Power — The Infernals
Melissa Uran

Okay, I'm still a fanboy at heart and the opportunity presented itself for me to get in touch with Adam Warren and hire him for a cover. I normally don't get that flabbergasted, but talking to him over the phone was amazingly rough. I love this man's art. From *Dirty Pair* to **Titans: Scissors, Paper, Stone** to his *Empowered* series to mention a few, I've read just about everything he's done. And now I have the opportunity to get him to do some work for me? Awesome. For each of his three covers, I gave him a basic outline, a few ideas of who/what type of creatures should show up on the cover and then just told him to cut loose and have fun. As you can see from the results, these covers are pure Adam Warren insanity at its best.

– BG

The Books of Sorcery, Volume V
— The Roll of Glorious Divinity II
Adam Warren

AUTOCHTHONIA

When the gods conspired to depose the Primordials, the Primordial Autochthon sided with the gods against his peers, having long been a target of their mockery for his ill health and unattractive form. It was Autochthon who first theorized the process of Exaltation and shared it with the gods. In addition, it was his Mountain Folk who provided the first Exalts with their mighty panoplies of arms that they might truly challenge the architects of Creation. After the war, however, the Exalts and gods found Autochthon's presence disturbing. He was a constant reminder of their base betrayal and a potential danger should he turn against the new status quo as he had the old. Realizing it was only a matter of time until the Exalted imprisoned or killed him like they had the other Primordials, Autochthon gathered his mortal worshipers within his very body and left Creation for the emptiness of Elsewhere.

Autochthon has dwelt apart from Creation ever since. His people live within his vast mechanized form, building a remarkably advanced civilization to rival those of the First Age in size and achievement. Recently, however, supplies of the magical materials the Autochthonians need to keep their world alive have run low. Having heard no word from their Machine God for many years, factions within Autochthonia have broken the seals that keep them from Creation in hopes of finding what they require there. What this means for both worlds remains to be seen.

This is a cross-section of the Primordial Autochthon, within whom dwell eight nations of people who retreated with the Great Maker to the Elsewhere beyond Creation in the early years of the First Age.

oil is Autochthon's lifeblood, and the vast pumps beneath the pole serve as his hearts

OIL

squid-like custodians swim in schools, mixing the lubricants as they scout their lightless inky realm

METAL

LIGHTNING

CRYSTAL

a complex the pole of as Autoch

SMOKE

the clouds of elemental smoke here are toxic and occasionally luminous

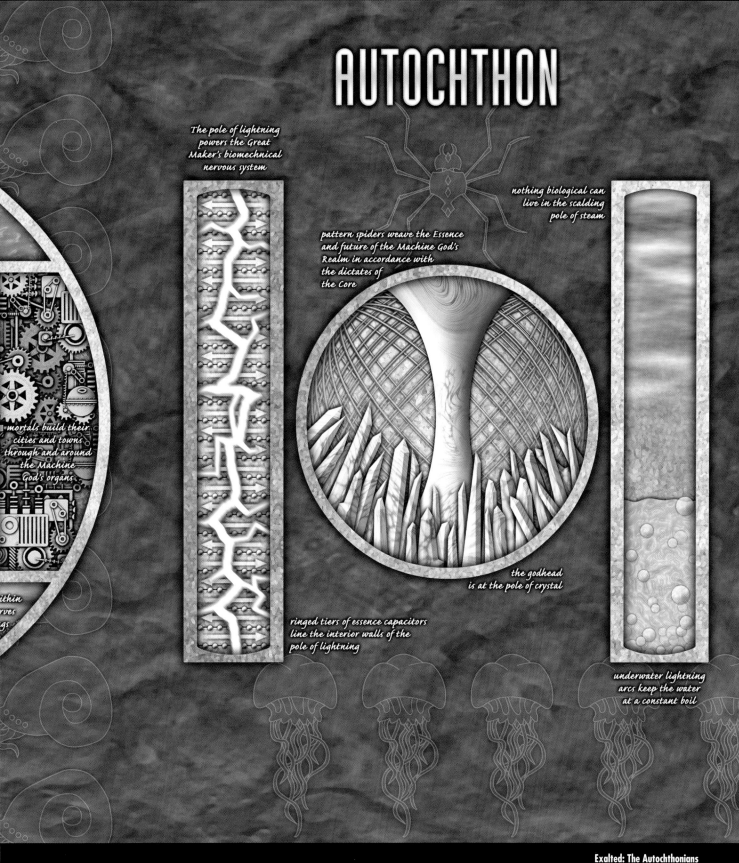

AUTOCHTHON

The pole of lightning powers the Great Maker's biomechanical nervous system

pattern spiders weave the Essence and future of the Machine God's Realm in accordance with the dictates of the Core

nothing biological can live in the scalding pole of steam

mortals build their cities and towns through and around the Machine God's organs

...ithin ...rves ...gs

ringed tiers of essence capacitors line the interior walls of the pole of lightning

the godhead is at the pole of crystal

underwater lightning arcs keep the water at a constant boil

Exalted: The Autochthonians
Ed Bourelle

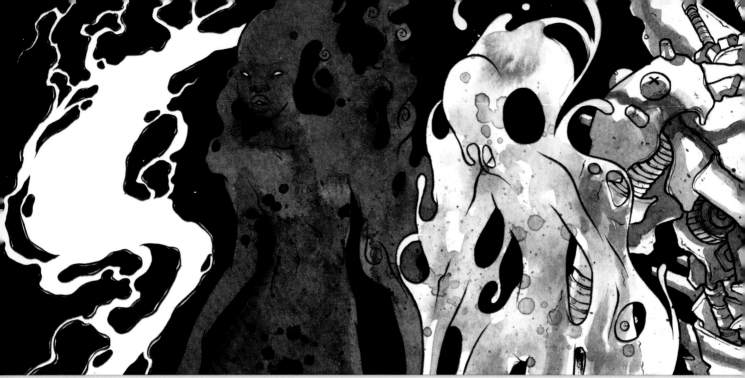

Exalted: The Autochthonians
Ross Campbell

Exalted: The Autochthonians
Jeff Holt

Exalted: The Autochthonians
Melissa Uran

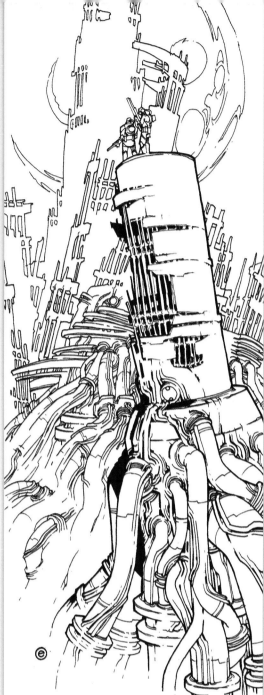

Exalted: The Autochthonians
Eric Canete

YU-SHAN

If Creation is a fortress built to keep the Wyld at bay, then Yu-Shan is the tower that crowns it. Built to accommodate the Primordials and their Games of Divinity, the Celestial City is now home to the mightiest of the gods and their ponderous Celestial Bureaucracy. The Bureaucracy is devoted to everything from the management of Creation's weather to the allotment of mortals' destiny. It is from Yu-Shan that the very Tapestry that makes up Creation is formed and where any mistakes in it are spotted and assigned to the Sidereal Exalted for correction.

The entire domed structure of Yu-Shan comprises a fabulous city the size and shape of the Blessed Isle. It contains enormous estates on which the greatest of gods live, immense heavenly bureaus where they work and the tremendous Jade Pleasure Dome, where the seven most powerful gods, the Incarnae, endlessly play the Games of Divinity. Those gods whom the Incarnae deem worthy are occasionally allowed to make a single move in the Games as a reward for their service, which is invariably the most transcendent experience in their immortal existences. None but the mightiest celestial gods and those who have legitimate business with them are even allowed to step foot in the city; even fewer gods are allowed to enter the Jade Pleasure Dome. In the entire history of Creation, few mortals have done the former and none has ever done the latter.

The Compass of Celestial Directions, Volume III — Yu-Shan
UDON

The Manual of Exalted Power — The Sidereals
Pasi Pitkanen

The Compass of Celestial Directions, Volume III — Yu-Shan
Justin Norman

Ruins of Rathess
Leanne Buckley

This was actually one of the harder places to illustrate.

How do you draw a place where the gods live and work, considering most of the gods don't even look human?

A place that's more full of bureaucracy and paperwork than your government. A magical, fantastic place, protected by giant lions made of gold, with quicksilver canals and cloud transports. Well, you just tell your artists to go nuts. You give rough descriptions to them and nudge them along in order to make a place so wondrous that your characters will try anything to get through one of the gates that lead to Yu-Shan. I think it turned out pretty good myself.

– BG

Games of Divinity
Adam Warren

The Books of Sorcery, Volume IV — The Roll of Glorious Divinity I
Adam Warren

Okay, we knew after we got this cover in that yes, it is a little sexist and it totally stoked the ExXxalted stories, but man, it's Hyung-Tae Kim. It's an amazing cover. He's never been known to really "reih it in", as an artist and I didn't want to limit him. The only major changes I had him fix were to cover her up a little bit and to get rid of her large elf ears. Also, this is the first cover where I've actually received physical hate mail about. But hey, publicity's a good thing, right? ;)

– BG

Savant and Sorceror
Hyung-Tae Kim

THE MANGA

Brian and I have had the good fortune to work with some of the most talented artists in the industry to produce what has become the signature of Exalted's second edition, its manga. When a new edition was being planned, both of us independently came to the design table with the idea of working actual manga pieces into the game. Word for word and panel for panel, I think these small one- to eight vignettes have done more to reveal the world of Exalted to the readers than any other facet of this edition. But why take my word for it, when the artwork speaks so eloquently for itself?

– JC

John and I were lucky to get the thumbs up to go with comic, or manga-style, chapter introductions. I think this has been really beneficial to the game line in showcasing the characters. You get a better feel for their personalities and hopefully some inspiration for your own game.

– BG

Dreams of the First Age
Andie Tong

Graceful Wicked Masques — The Fair Folk
Imaginary Friends Studio

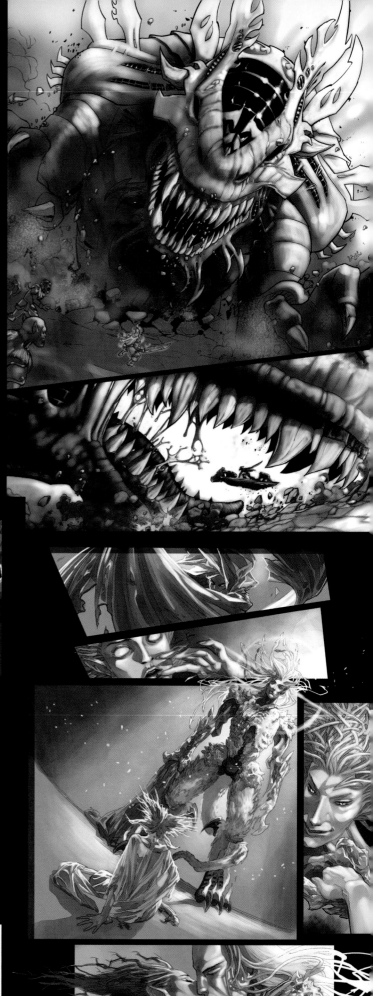

I've been lucky to work with so many incredible artists over the years.

I still feel like a kid in a candy shop over the fact that I get to hire all this great talent and make these cool books for all of you. It's amazing how tight-knit the art community is. So many of my artists know each other, so it's just easy for me to be able to hire them and know I'm going to get good, solid work out of them. I've made so many friends these past seven years that I couldn't even begin to list them all. In fact, just go take a look at the credits page. Be sure to read through all the art credits. These guys and gals (and so many more that we just didn't have the room to include in the book, regrettably) define **Exalted**. They provide visual inspiration to the players of this fine game and to other artists. I can't thank management enough for the decision to change the art style all those years ago and for entrusting me with the visual look of this game. I also can't thank you, the reader, enough. The fact that you love this game so much is the reason I'm here and do this. Thank you for letting me give you a little peek behind the scenes of these cool images over the years from my talented pool of artists. I hope you all continue to love **Exalted** as much as I do.

– BG